When Thy King Is A Boy

When Thy King Is A Boy

Poems by

Ed
Roberson

University
of
Pittsburgh
Press

Acknowledgment is made to the following publications in which some of the poems in this book first appeared: *Atlantic Monthly, Ideas and Figures, May We Speak, Nomos,* and the *Pittsburgh Point.*

The Detroit Artists Workshop first published "few" and "sole irrhythm" in *Work.*

"18,000 feet," "true we are two grown men," "romance," "suite," "the only night in town," "if the black frog will not ring," "queue," "report," and "layout job" were first published in *New Directions 22,* © 1970 by the New Directions Publishing Corporation.

The quotation on p. 70 is from "Chapter III, Jim" in *The Heads of the Town up to the Aether* by Jack Spicer, copyright 1962 by Jack Spicer.

*Publication of this book
has been aided by a grant
from
the A. W. Mellon
Educational and Charitable Trust.*

Contents

When Thy King Is A Boy

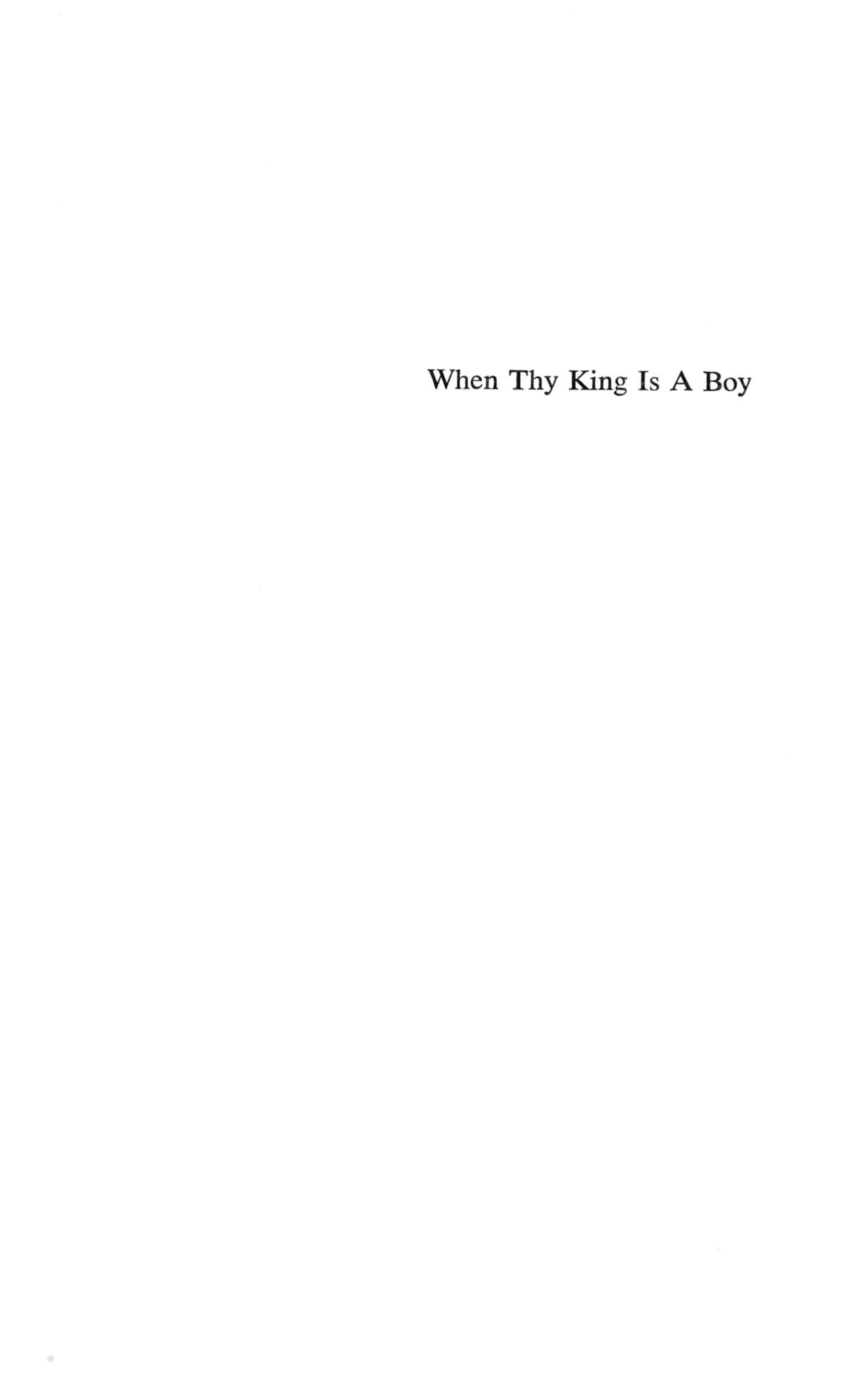

Woe to thee, O land, when thy king is a boy,
And thy princes feast in the morning.

Eccles. 10:16

those few last days that clear before the snow
slowly fogs off the neat edge of the field
behind the school from buildings all the way
downtown almost.   those days that clear enough
to let us see how far up the leaf smoke
goes.   during those days something happened.
i saw it first because i was allowed
outside to play before you were.   i waited
so it wouldn't fly away before you came.
and when you did you cried.   but you were smaller.
and when it did not move or go away
we knew the things to do.   the jars of mud
hidden around the yard that were supplies
against the germans in our wars we put
together underneath the porch.   the guns
were yours and you returned my helmet and
while someone called we buried all our rings
and my uncle's two red bars.   then went
inside.   for bed i washed my whole self clean
put on my favorite underwear and prayed
twice because i had forgot to say
goodbye to you.   and like always it
is day it   is day it is night
as if nothing had happened but everyone
knows who the black bird without feathers
on its red neck is.   so all night i wait.

I

there is against explicit stating what things are
the family of instants born to a happening,
the multiple thunder of the number of their hearts:
the fly buzzing against the window and the plane
that for the lack of just that character
somewhere is going down.   there is a child somewhere
who screams in an amusement park   whose hands,
begging the heavens for this balloon,   have just dispatched
the dark zeppelins against the english night.
and in the countryside the circumstance
adds a spoon of dull explosion to the tea
and at the same time in france there falls a rain
adding to what already is without any relation
except perhaps the stupid sea
the continents move in . . .

II

i am afraid that some hand not my own
may rise and answer present to my name,
that some me might debate me on this button
i have been careless these years pinning on,
leaving an unowned grasp its emptiness.
i am afraid my fine foot may not answer
'slender' 'warm' slow arched one of these mornings
as it should, because it had awakened
here too soon.   taking one early step
into tomorrow tomorrow i am not in.

Thirteen Poems From The Two Andes

(*for Larry*

1

all night down the palms
       slithers.
all quiet. fluent with mooneggs.
      the scribble
            of the trees
    is   the wind.
the only witness.   now
that only once articulate
      echo has used his word
      in the dark.

2

wide   eyes.   the spots   on wakened jaguars
wink from where   the sun's noughts tally
up in the trees   until a whole
        cat   dawns in the open.

3

the one plane   like the only sun
brings life to the jungle   sets
down toward the potted growth
of buildings without routes in
or out
      the high cheek of the hill
tattooed the provider's pattern
by the dot drawn crowd stiffens:
it rolls into them on their airstrip
            tongue

4

their tree faces have horded in
the tattoos underneath their eyes
that just were all of them   gathered

to see the strange clicked tongue
the one stepped from the sunfaced plane
speaks with   when he speaks

they stare into his mouth and eyes.
the town has given him
the only other aluminum roof

besides the one god has in case
the strange constriction in his mouth
should drop down from its tree of teeth

and swell full in tomorrow's sun
great with their sin of hanging on
their sisters the rootless orchids

5

where no one else
has been or been
and died o holy
holy becomes the message
of my latest footprint

6

a lizard's back   the dry mountains)
weaves across the caked sky
ahead of the snaking heat

7

    by the press the laundress sun is
    the sky is starched too tight
    the cattle pop out of their meat
    and long ago the clouds out of their milk

8

                ahead   is the mane.
                behind, the tail.
                both are the road.

9

    where the ridge   twitches
                the fly)   the bus (is
    drones from spot to spot   which)
                the tail pesters

10

                the two nuisances
                with a slap:panorama!
                the hills fanned with hugeness
                the wing of buses
                egged back to minutia
                    lay still

11

    near homilies of idleness
    the road whines
    up within the ticking

    tossing of stones
    against the undercarriage
    the sharp redundant

switchbacks   on the way intrude
that feather

sticking the distant nightmare
into the bundled fabric
of sleep

the dream of going over
the edge   of the idleness of falling
from the arms of terror the tantalization
                              of a hard
                              on waking up

12

once a month a bus goes over
the horse whose eyes hang out)
the edge. races down a thousand feet
the horse whose eyes hang out
the dead balls of its potent tongue
the horse whose eyes hang out
seeing the black rider   fills the road
with the horse   whose eyes hang out
the headon stare of death and him embrace

13

the dusts lay in the hot air
as a crowd just adjourned from noon
a congregation that has lifted
itself partway up
from its bed of chairs
and stares loveless back at what
has just been said
                        eyes
less occupied than thin roach shells
emptied by those brittle aisles of death.

8

it has scratched shadows
angels that meant its passing   on my gate
it has bent down my stalk of sun
until the bloom breaks off behind the hill
it has stuck wads of breath into
a toy man sickness had played with
one game after another
and it has looked in one man's eye
and was not seen to walk away

what has gone on with it behind the doors
that, closed off, define me in this building
i am jealous of
and print upon the door
                    a hall is spent
taking what we are called between us yet

its boot crossing the same field
          has brought to mud
the hard earth finally
a day nothing can get through but that it enters

i must be careful about such things as these.
the thin-grained oak.   the quiet grizzlies scared
into the hills by the constant tracks squeezing
in behind them closer in the snow.   the snared
rigidity of the winter lake.   deer after deer
crossing on the spines of fish who look up and stare
with their eyes pressed to the ice.   in a sleep.   hearing
the thin taps leading away to collapse like the bear
in the high quiet.   i must be careful not to shake
anything in too wild an elation.   not to jar
the fragile mountains against the paper far-
ness.   nor avalanche the fog or the eagle from the air.
of the gentle wilderness i must set the precarious
words.   like rocks.   without one snowcapped mistake

how these loose rocks got piled up here like this
when everything below builds up so steadily—
        a swoop a day long countries wide increases
        from deeper green into a paler leaning
        ice   then to this small pile and finally
        to room for each of us one at a time
        careful   of the cracking of the flag.
how piece by piece   stepped beyond   the element
of left and right   taken away, the sense of here
is made   all there is
under the feet,   all to come down
how much a prison freedom is
to what is   i
                        learned

lakes so long that they upend   into
some ridged wave   there in that moment
tall enough to crest the sun's last rays
when all the other waters lay in darkness.
valleys deep enough the clouds that set
their rainfeet in the bottom grass can stare
only the broadways that the gamest eagles
dare   face to face to watch themselves
        upon the mountain
fine as a fog drop   work their way again
(as in a dream before their own huge eye)
        into a thunderhead . . .

        what was i remembering
        the avenue extends across the street
        and goes uphill only a couple blocks.

. . . the one lake on the whole
            peninsula that does not freeze
is this one.   where it turns
where the two arms down two alleys
of mountains meet and startle one another
at the corner   ships went down
during the goldrush when the water was highway
to what men dregged out of the earth
    to landings not built on the land.

on the ridge behind   a line wound up,
the ranger said, to an abandoned mine.
the men went in the cars came out
the donkeys brought it down
and the succession had only begun.
if the current didn't swallow the ship   drinking
the pockets the cards whirl it round into
the dancing   the women the strict maelstrom
between their legs   that brought them back:
the men went in . . .
                the cars from the army base
come down so often.
the boys on leave pile out go in
to work the old swollen vein.
and the water still the same can change
its face in a matter of minutes
the current   monster
to listen to the gold built up to be thrown in
to the same old hole . . .

        what do i keep remembering
        that makes this bitch keep asking me
        where my mind is.   (the boat)
        i'm not that drunk and yet the whole joint rocks
        around beneath me   the whole deck
        down in this hold the animals lean out their stalls
        and roar
                and now
                        it comes
        to me. (the music) i remember

the evening i got really scared
to think that i had been gone months.
someone could be really sick and days
someone back home be hurt and days
i could die and days
days would pass before the flood of incidents ran off
and left my body days old anywhere.
i started back to camp and it was then
i came on the boat wrecked   thrown
into the trees   huge hornets rats and weasels
in it.   on its side: ARK II.
in camp the rangers knew   they all were proud
it was too perfect.
we all got drunk that night but i
felt the same need i feel now
to go inside and pack
and get back against a wall away
from whatever hole   i hear opening in the floor.

true we are two grown men
beyond the wand-length of magical things
and sting of the crazy-berry thorns.
but this bend is what we turn lately back into. where
the trains S close to the river
where we mad used to play.
our after school has been these years.
for you, a wife; for me, the want
of what we always came
here for anyhow, come now
again hunting to commit
before our weak each end-outrage.

coming on behind the clock work
of their engines march the cars
like minutes to throw life at.
we watch the thing throw up the spark
that stones do round about sunset

true we are two grown men
for whom time's wild caboose too soon
will wave away our chance to lay
our heads our wooden eyes
spite-wide upon the railroad tie
and watch the thunderous universe
of will pass so near over us
coach after raging coach.

dreaming has made more strict the terms
of dreaming.   the coinage of confusion
in towers i regret is spread
on an expensive bed.   the difference
becomes a harder thing to purchase
                    at the market evening
some forms are shown to be those of the moon
now whore to habits that were
                    once free with a darkness.
a used to be light   cutting off
tying down or not allowing in
has had a dream's hangers ripped away
and by the terrible tradition that is
creates the term of eunuch for what is to be.
                    o buyer
what is on the mind is not easy
to come right out and tell you   certain things
and dreams not finished to the point
of final polished starting up   and screaming
            sat up in bed all at once
dull   ended in no dream at all.
            except the one
that it was   on there hard   whatever it was.
to tell you   sits you
                    up too
                    dulls you
                    ends you know
because there are no certain things.
because to dream is not to dream
            if waking up is never finished
            the terms never fulfilled.

of some i know   that do get up
their trains roll in from countries that i know
are just outside of town, they break in seacaves
underground and send the foam up through
the streets.   a certain chair will catch their pants
and hold their bodies all from floating back
until the evening tide books out again.
and in this building i can feel my toes
brush in its dandruff beach twenty floors deep
and sometimes in their path crush something soft
out of a fragile hidden shell.
of some i know   a shell i know
from now on will obediently roll out
and back along a channel   made of this
            move of this attraction
for children to pick up and study   silence
for its wives who when it gets home   take
            it naked coiled and coral-skinned
into their bed and hold it folding softly round it
            call in   to come out   what she wants
            out of the shell.
until—when all that neaps out is the wave
that small girls tricked by old men hear   she'll scream
empty her head of tears upon the pillow
            holding the dead thing to her
            swear she heard him   in there.
of what i know   this is no where
            i'm going. though . . .

"a place for seeing   a long ways away
the clouds puff over the corner of the earth
and line car after car after the engine
wind has roared on by, a place to wave
at the space being carried off at the day being done
so openly   the fast shadows in the wheat
                getting away . . ."
with this   runaways wrap up their change estate
to put on when they meet the king   a shirt
other bums in the sided car have not walked over.
an apology of dragons for the tardy knight
          shutting down his failed crusade
in the hours before the dawn of this other era.
          another scheduled   passing.

dreaming has made so strict the terms
that dreaming is had by thieves
bought with what is not dreamed a dream,
on a street that is a set up   the rest
          the old   the is   of the rest
of the week standing in judgment of the theft
          is each   nothing
each loose hanging end's end
the coin that disappears the whore the moon that wasn't
          there.

the cold has put blue horses where lambs were.
and quiet cows that fattened in the night
upon the grass are driven in and stones
wild veined with ice have taken over in
the fields: the moon is chewing on the snow.
and something watching from a stand of pines
has tied off screams into a hanging knot

the road has spent the night of winter clean
of passengers: the thread out of the hills
has helped the naked trees remain in love
on their bare bodies.   the decent leaves unmade.
and nothing warm has passed inside the gate
to say a word against the solid well
nor the bucket cord that does not weave its drink.

there is a man who, if he cried, the hard
rare droppings of the wolves digesting hunger
would tear his grunting eyes: who, if he spoke,
the shrill fillings of dead men's teeth could cut
his gums with silences they know, who lives
nine valleys from the sun, who if he loved—
would simply love and roll from her unnoticed
        by her arriving immigrant bees.

it is now known why the farmers
desert that fondling of their fields
why their wives give up the chickens
to the sly night that ferrets
the moon egg in the trough from between
the legs of the fence it is now
known why the children are hushed in
behind the lamps and the horses
excuse themselves into inconspicuous tufts
in the field's sleep because
it is embarrassing
this romance of empty space
that makes the open smell
of cowshit so untouchably near
that the white silo on the next farm
sweats with moonlight and accidentally
spills a slight stream of corn

the cat floats in that frigate hunch upon the floor
the heater low upon the rug horizon burns
this winter doldrum sealed and still as drapery
the hall's imagined rug runs equatorial
from sleep to food to sleep again an endless east
unless the day enters the turning back
puts toward the pole not to get up again
to watch the bladders turn to salt and crack inside
    the hold strangling the day's first bud of slavery

the cat opens the drapes split up their folded eye
a napped sun stretches downward to the floor with fangs
the bluish fur of gas is up and hisses heat
and rubbed against the window lints the pane with sweat
the closed door sleeps the same roost in the wall as always
on the egg here is unless the feline
hours of habit howl the winged door off
what has been hatching in the dark and takes the morning
      all its skin to put it out into its cinder

young men's trousers are so firm
they show their groins and all the young
fluency of their quick knees.
but old men o the lapsing crease
the bulgy varicose of thread
so wide the many montaged limbs
of age's tremor all have room
a private fold to waste in.

firm the young girl's breasts are raised
so clear above the vague climaxes
of her belly that the pimples
on her points count off like saints.
like flattened chapels the old women
are out-miracled by their grave
conception of a time so deep
its monumental weaning pulls
their teats down out of sight.

eclipse

i am not a handsome man
women do not tell me
the slither of my muscles cause
their private hearts to itch,
i have the least long handsomeness
to me and that is time.

the route i take across the roofs
does not bring out the flags
of girls who trolley out their laundry
waving down the honey man.
the winged pennants of the sun
and i hit the street

separate and quiet hunting
for someone.   and i
having less range, stay on this earth-
sun, i too have missed moons)
and missed being crossed together
in the unhideable

and brilliant obscuring of the hole.

I

i

the white teeth of the nigger moon grin off the wall.
i am about to be told something coldly
that i have buttoned on no pants even
no close word underwear against
what somewhere off the cap of greenland
drums must be breaking up:
    great grey ice pulls waveless into view.

ii

she seemed taller than i was
only because my eyes were lower
than her hair piled up to be.
her face was small her neck was long
and ending proudly in her nose
the way i always wanted
that pharaohess to me
to be hawk boned.
i kept talking looking down
at how her housedress opened
high over her thighs
but did not speak the notice.
and in the later of its room
and desert sleep is egypt;
and the falling pyramid out of my brain
that through my throat, my chest, has dreamed
to stab my genitals . . .
i wake. i bathe. i am ashamed
at what my god has done
to dam and hurt this nile:
its eddies curdle, toads hump stones,
it cannot get its reeds to stand up straight.

iii

all the unstraight surface of a sphere
is held accountable for curving for leaping
from the mother right and the father left
and from the placeless early point of god.
and all the plane-wild skin responsible
for rounding me, (firm young, flaccid with age
that only clocks sequenced from hard to soft
gossip about) owes me of heats and cold.
but something long behind in its duty
something fed and bathed is in my house
of bones that does not tell the turns it takes
give its alarms nor sound its explode questions
and because of it the truth is so unge-
ometrical i jag on the gates of horn.

it not just occurs to me but comes
like fever; i have never seen your breasts,
that in these times of low exposure i
remain most dressed complete to yet my glasses
and speak "the old high love" from no sore known
but to book fools   (the body's summers cannot
be so easily antidot'd nor wiped—
and it not just occurs but is disease.
disease that opening will unveil the nipple
even from your shelves and show the milky
cells the bright bees label "this for love."
disease to scab away the word, the learned
illusion from the lip that sentences
the mind: disease to make my hand's touch new.

II

i

owners of what they own
under the unescapable
deed of singular skin
ask their two genetic salesmen who
have watched the plot that they by two had let
break and escape
what country they are in.

the sea has stolen grain by grain
the letters of the sand
the breakers can be heard deciding
formally the order of the vowels.
and simply as the hours play into night,
through the walls
the son has robbed his father's bed
eaten the plundered and become like him.
the striking amulets on his belly.

a name unweaves on reaching the intestines.
the title of the kingdom still unknown.
for all his violence,
the headdress unidentified . . .

ii
straightened from the sleep the form of egg
the chin is lifted from the clavicle
into the upright of its pride the pillow
of the chest is stuffed with musculature
and air has laid its head on it.
now the years have put them to expect
the orbs to be their potent, the sceptre
its damascus of perfection, these
together a right,—

iii
  the legs are such precarious things
exposed foundations ivyed down with hair
the casings rock has evolutions over
deserted and left bare.
time will termite into them
and chance flood them under accident.
on champions the formal masonry
is prone to come unmarried at the seams
the loose torso upon the seasonless bough
   heavily intestined with dark worms.
i am a lot concerned about my body.
all its rooms.   and all the rhythms tapped
out on its walls that answer back
            in moving
the trapped in occupant toward death.
the sole irrhythm in the brain
never answering why.

III

i

                    to have hands
one on the arms of old maids in their beds
the other finally gallantly at the door
of a carriage no one hears pull off
then one, long idle, i have seen cloud over
the cold laugh of the moon at me   him
it has sat up in the night out of safe dreams
to question what he wants so not to
to do against himself that asks the value

ii

the times are such you should not love a man
beyond acquaintance.   yet the struggled arm
you grip the trembling same crutch with, your hand
under the tabled world shackled to
yourself to ask it its hysteric extremes
is so much beautiful and like my own
that when you knock the fixtures from the place
that's set for prides like ours in your collapse,
the other knights i am around the table
sit silent and not question your release
your rhythm   nor the oracle you've heard
who answers you here far out in the outposts
of yourself immediate when all
the other women are countries away in town.

iii

. . . there is a corner just ahead whose turning
is so badly understood that being
upset is included in the tickets.
the beauties of the track are well known words,
the lines which evenings run gold to the sun.
but just inside the glare—the cornering:
the architecture of its wreckages
a depot out of nowhere with its hook
to make the harshest of transactions with the parcels
down from the naïve hills.
the coaches come and on them
all the peopling of the one-eyed race,
so many beardless pelts compartmented
to make the business of the merchant flies
so easy in the last bazaar of spoilage in the sun

iv

one corner short of the horizon

IV

i

i wear less until i'm down to naked.
it gets hotter the closer that it gets.
the sky has lapsed. the smoke is near my head
the cinder. and the flame is down between
my legs from sitting on the cold cold moon
watching the moths make love. o it gets hotter
closer that it gets, truer without
its games, to being miserable summer.
the things undress. their signs along the road
undress the word the next page past the law's
allowance keeping the pointing mileage clear.
and i am finding out, i am arriving
male and baggageless at the august truth
where for a room i am assigned a stone.

ii

i was so naked
my bones in danger
of peeling to the crustless marrow
that i simply
asked her she said
yes.
    and fattened me with her body.
muscled with her wire hair
far as we could
we lifted ourselves to see the morning.

1

the news is covered

today brought to you
by the same coverage

as smothered yesterday

There is this to say
there is no stillness
if there is a voice

announcing this
is stillness
It is broken i have broken

this piece just to still
closer to stillness
An Absence

2

in its   role as an important part
in the play of time information has
the latest word has been pronounced dead.

causes are that cause as what was felt
to first have moved the feeler to the subject
he is now is not to be performed

object   on which the bug movements of interest
weave a coverage and lay opinions
towards a blossoming that bursts with time

and time's diversity of rots

3

    it can never be said
    a mob was made by this
    voice with its intension
    in delivery
    so it can never be said
    we return you now
    to the news with any truth

4

    the news is brief
    as air   as light
    as paper is how it arrives
    tho it is all the headstone

    this population of voice
    and ancient filigreed face
    of type concerns
    you   with you

5

    top official for the purposes
    of top   security has released
    lies   defining a position
    the whirl of balances will even
    not let stand

             on his side
    the this side   up points on
    to the horizon as the subject
    turns and backs out of sight

rescue workers fought today
and yesterday another day today
in efforts to avert the same
tomorrow. one eye witness on the scene
reported and the wide effects
opened a decade in the wrecks
of sequences supposed under control.
official estimates of toll
have been suppressed for purposes of piece
by piece attention to belief.
authorization to the area
is given as is birth to myriads.

skin that is a closed   curtain.
it is impossible to know.   how
the light is cast.

a mark that is kept   the elect-
ion determining the race
before the candidate   runs.

darkie is the night is
an old image given color.
the skin is history.the dark horse

they are made to stand side by side
the black lawns of their toes to the curb.
though we who know the nakedness of mind
might not call them naked   they are naked
in the cold   stripped to what comes

before and holds the mind. their attic heads
except for those rare spots where warmth is thought
gathered beneath their struts   are beaten
white with snow   and snow's fine lash
delineates the brick hairs on their chests.

icicles drop from what the windows see
inside and out across the street   icicles
what the door addressed answers in turn
when underground the bestial root system
of supply's demands face them unpaid.

those mothers down there off the hill
don't pray to the mother.
saturday is a man's day.
that's who they are.

son when you rise
don't come back here.
you are too light to make it
so dark around here.

god your father one day
or another   another day
the sunday of a friday night
that's who you are.

week without that day.
off, some mothers
has to carry evenings up the hill
to make it   dark.

we cruised the block a couple times
        to wait the space
my car parked at your curb   signs:
        we used your place.
we fed your pets and   each other)
        someone else's.
things were taken care of. rather
        chance they'd smell this
on us we picked up our rings
        from your tub.
we will have left behind some things.

        pursing our stubs
the wrinkle of attendance covers
        our played parts
living in one man's house and another's
        parts.

the change of blankets was observed
the green as usual
was lovely
trees as is the taste of trees
wore cotillion qualities of sweetness.

males on females forced earrings
of phone receivers modishly
supplying what's in season.

and dressed in undress for the heat
is how   arranged
i'd come to meet
this habit of new grass the dowdy
spring of last years' love had not yet thrown:

the change from my cold bed to our
hot nature is a season
we who've died before   should not have seen.

he went into   his room that no one there
and somehow open   closets   held his suits
his suits like him   held no one not even
the racks because like that the hold is nulled
the his of his suits' shoulders closed around
the fragile her
                of metal fine except
she is his bone and he the style she wears.
he closed   the empty door no one behind him
since it was not her   and closed the closet.
what the
            Police unhung yesterday
and folded must have been   was him only
in his shorts as if his suits were stolen.

he has come to sleeping with his clothes
on   somewhere around the unfed waste
of his mind he wears the slight depression
of a home like a skinny jew.
he has come to holding with attention
something she must ask him to set down
to take her up if just against his bones
(which some place else is honing to a blade.
it has come to listening between
them between their words to each other
a bitter cloth of singleness' last knot.
on his tongue waits else   where like a porter
it has come the passes from his brain
across his eye/kiss   rivers) dry goodbye.

hole for female fills the term
for what is what. between us runs
the meanest tie time passes on.
and we are down to narrow rails
about each other.   come together
only in the darkened distances.

and male is fill and empties us
landscaping our desire.
over nothing   live open
the metal teeth. the dark mushroom
licks out. it, eden's occupant
in me   through you sucks its own   poisoned lips.

the only night in town
operates one bar
in all the districts of its hours
this one establishment

the cheaper stars of glasses
set up shorter destinies
inside dream than dream's
dry open country

corked encompassed   seconds
line the bar up to the time
one breaks off the last note
of the loud high of a dime

in her ear   someone
clear enough the music
lets it reach the walls' gossip
of opposing mirrors

that the dead spot partnerless
on the floor goes as far
on as it comes   from
the only night in town

1

if the black frog will not ring
  it's the telephone
i promise   my fingers
for its wart garden afruit with noise
and so much touch the civilization
cannot get its thumbs into its ears.

and it is wrong to go to bed and stay
and it is wrong to stay awake and play
                you didn't hear it so
again it is wrong
it is always wrong.

the frog's night
is the black night turned over   under covers
from the sun at both noons
the flashes before the eyes, squeezed tight,
are twenty moons   the tightness makes
the ears ring.

and it is wrong not to be home
and it is wrong to be someplace
                else   an unreached party
or the wrong
address.   me always as the wrong

2

exchange.   within the black frog's night
is the brand eyed dog
going from lance to lance to piss
upon the body

the skeletal trees   brittle reeds
the municipal legged insect
of streets   webs together

the will o' wisp of talk
pole to pole to somewhere
somewhere makes the black frog sing

the fly is dying hard
he is dreaming

his back has hit
the underside of heaven

he is a drill
instead of a spade

i am a monkey
man. not a babfoon

.armed for the first
time against the last

kindling floor of your dreaming

it is for your own safety you must stand
back from the window.   outside is about to go
off again.   the edgy wall reflections and
the corner patterns are signals which i know
by now by heart by sheltered heart.   the snappish red
and green   light in the fallow ceiling's plastic bath
(that is the dollar ten cent chandelier so deadened
with the algae of the night) like birds of wrath.
it is not considered that you know the world.
you must stand in the silver garden globe
where you'll be told.   the main side of the room will break.
make no outcry.   at times this launch of ends has hurled
a still green seeing eye through here.   if it probes
its own distortion in your crystal   make it wait.

the red ass of the screaming mandrill sun
shuts off where the trees close behind
it with the sky. the guards of light dragged off.
the hands washed of the day wear their blood
close to the skin only a short time then
wearing a glass and gestures light a friend
in those mouths   the tribal semi-circle
                    smear of smiles

the grass (his honed the even edge is worn
around by his house like the robes of oracles.
the words directed by the dark   open
their yellow eyes: the light is on the hunt
for reign over these gathered   houses' suns.
his silver feeds their dark of confidences
nakedness   he's made. deadly perfect
                    invitation of the moon

he feeds on eyes like neon moths that read.
and of blindness stars brighter foliage.
he drags the judges of their senses off
to glories where they can't see what he is
or burns or why because each new taste turns
its what the sweet life is his fruit remains
the flowering not enough.   he like the sun
                    unable to either drop or eat the light.

The pill to stay up dropped him through its arms.
and he has spent its time in its lost bed.
and it   down on its hands and knees in nightmare
on his chest   could still not find his eyes.
and this means that   this morning when it dies
before the hour squad of the sun   run out,
the project   still   undone is its white carcass
on the desk without a line of life.

The sun has fired and his bright job is dead.
and sweating in his undressed suit he lies
where he fell   shirted and tied excuse.
blank morning finally blackens his name
to night time itself pills with time yet on

His hands and knees he finds his corpse to draw on.

a week at once of all the passengers
he is at daily getting in to work
had stood and motionless let us go by.
the next day every head on board pretended
guilty interest in this single empty
lot familiar only for a second
time as where a fellow stop is lost.
then friday all the years he'll miss at once
stood at his stop and stared at ours continuing
to mondays' separation by the passing lane.

there is a fox growing in my field
so many flowers so many leans of wind
so many not so risings of the land
the bones hanging out its mouth.

so many times in a winter night
two blue horses of the moon
lie down die and ride
up under the legs of my shadow.

there is a here growing in my road
so many triangles so many narrows of the point
so many solitary houses on the distance
losing to its abstract fire.

no one could have a blacker tail
or whiter tie in contrast on
than me.   the face of the evening guests
is some shade earlier than darkness
which is my countenance.   i bring
your daughter in the arm of midnight
she knows that i eat orchids with
my fingers.   she has seen unnapkined
my whole greedy primitive body.
and she wiped it with her hair
and when i smiled she said how proud
she was that i was always dressed.
for dinner.   if i sneer in the sheets at night
my tie becomes crooked but do not
be alarmed i am well mannered.

the subject was reported seen
facing a window at what seemed
to be a late reflection.

proprietors deny the window
or that anything at all
is in it anyhow.

a witness has been found who cost
his findings which were lost
among his life

but whose holdings are not official.
victims are advised
to pass or be satisfied.

When Thy King Is A Boy

I

i frog prince have sunk more into the change
than the simple dip of love or coin
those ungreen clods mudfill the wish vein with.
green i leaned in like these need never try.
the small kiss that a frog has   taken in
the moon's face on the water   breaking up
and swallowing the coin i am thrown in.
no wish not even practice love   granted
me.   only the well's slug of my lasting
green and lack returned me.   me taken
in that hand those having are not dealt
by that sharp   intact they needn't meet
that term they filthily them   needn't try striking.

i frog prince in my poorness put to change
more that a wealthless organ and a face.
a whole estate of what wishes could be
wished from all i could be as a frog.
left this miscoined patience   i am.
after all a prince   eventually.
she came

(amor vincet omnes, sleeping beauty!

there never comes the so desired beginning
that somewhere does not trip in its procession
somewhere that won't include mis-invitations
to a few slow legged drawbacks who string
the liberation to continuum.
there never sounds a bell that does not bring
the old hour with it or the minute thing
of its old rule that swings it soon back dumb.
the sure event to make things different
is come and so much better than believed
has done itself.   but one love in its bed
does not law love the prick machine of these
bubbles of to be undone worlds nor wed
that stiff win to the after it has spent.

(nudum pactum

what i do love will prove just enough
til more than what enough was when we tried
our cause is committed by its done.
i will set worlds right in your bed tonight
i have your look and see that says that done
is precedent   that do the only source.
i have your look   and see that read that read
and read   leaks how the lien on love is done.
but when i end over into sleep
what plaintiff of a lover underneath
our world has not had his and sues toward ours.
what full one doesn't ends us shy because
no one who knew knows why when it has done
doing what does   it was not what to do

IV

1

The king has fallen to the raw belief
in women for his ills.   and time is ill
            to him. so naked
on the table lies the state
in its affairs   and balanced tendencies
            it takes to grip a woman
while the hemorrhoid hunter has his finger
            chambered in the puzzle

of the lay anatomy.   it is
believed the two are covered under one
            embracing policy
after which unarmed arrangement naked
            on the table rests
in its flagging insurances the state
            of impotence and dragging
beauty tripping on its (40's) was.

twentyone: they were once. they two bared
for each others' stethoscopic nip
            of breast—but that is over.
it has fallen to the raw belief
that rung, its grabbing up calls living
            to the line   out of
the smart or moldy snatch of talk.
and it has come   to this.

56

2   two bitches.

3

under the subtle pimp of silken
organization   girlishly fell the state
        in patients' dream
of safety   into danger in the sheets
        of taken care of
businesses only the proper undoing
gets done and retaped in the red knot of want not
        taken care of

under the supple silk of pimping
organizing its mannishness feels the state
        under mons veneris
of tape its real anatomy   and hates
        the smooth new bed it has
erected to its swollen office

4

stabs itself on this disorder
        palms off
the joseph's blood for wedding stains

convenes its ancestral physicians
        with a pride
of flags all roaring maned

lies down and waits the upshot
        of the fall
from the mount.   already named
        the (grievish) father.

5

The king before the king all their long night
        had not become the father
of the future he had thought.   the son
        remained unknown.
and by the heavy walk of the clouds
of his own doubt
                it could not be forecast
        if the sun so late carried
        so high might not be blackened hell.

and we have entertained his nakedness
with just that other bitch of his own
        nakedness.
probing its own probe all their long night.

6

and it has come to this

                simply the king
                has put his night in.
                applied to a wound
                inside himself.

                that he knows
                is the cunning window the
                        mystery
                all he is come thru.

7

The only
social object is
"a man, carved
out of himself"

and under that
stone
the state miscarries.

8

"And it shall be assigned unto.
You shall find   to come   conspicuous
enough, lying in the moment
king . . ."

9

Now there came to the king the questioner
and asked if it were day or were it night.
the king looked in the mirror at the son
and said he was himself. as for his own
he could not say who owned the crown or where
inside the nigger mirror his line hid.
the questioner walked in him to his bath
and floated in his lap. and its one eye
dry of the glances it had hit him with
turned to the queer as he thought she came in.

he hung his towel and ended toward the day
                of business with the state.

jacket

many of these poems attempt to make
happen to words   that which happens
to lines

                 in an optical illusion
many of these lines have.   that.

kind of architecture of
things which live   in the sea
they are built
,without a base
beginning above
the ordinary ground of the mind
and ending   there in
illusion

yet they are not
illusions   they are
real because the poetic of all (our languages
has the more potential for concretion
it can be said that

"Many of these poems attempt to make
happen to words that which happens
to lines in an optical illusion.
Many of these poems have that.
kind of architecture of
things which live in the sea
They are built without a base.
beginning above

the ordinary   grcund of the mind
and ending   there in
illusion.Yet   they are not illusions. They are
real because   the poetic of all our languages
has the more potential for concretion.
It can be said that either these poems
 recognize   their suspension so clearly
concretize   their suspension so graphically
OR from   their suspension
 recognize   the ground   so clearly
that the glareglarity/clarity of that vision
has created
 such   a solid about itself that that.
chaos   is the real ground."—Mr. Roberson
writes—Ed Roberson is not a real poet.
and further: Many of these poems attempt to make happen to words
that which happens to lines in an optical illusion. Many of these
poems have that kind of architecture of things which live in the
sea. They are built without a base, beginning above the ordinary
ground of the mind and ending there in illusion. Yet they are not
illusions. They are real: because the poetic of all our languages has
the more potential for concretion. It can be said that either these
poems recognize their suspension so clearly, concretize their suspen-
sion so clearly, or from their suspension recognize their ground so
clearly that the glare (regularity/clarity) of that vision has created
a solid about itself such that chaos is the real ground.

Mr. Roberson,
from the Preface
to The Next Song

the old woman   of the night
                       who knows   so much

the old woman   of the line before the night
                       who gives us to her daughter

the old woman   of the dark
                       who looks into our baby sleep
                       that we are well
                       of all terror but her black and oldness

the old woman   of the light who is silver
                       on the first shining of our skin
                       for the rusty wars of flesh
                                                 so much

the old woman   of our suns
                       who walk her in a blue cloth
                       smaller than her body
                       her white hair held above a thousand family heads
                       her feet the old black mountains
                       river soled and on their way

                       to a dance
of old women   who give us to a daughter's daughter
                                 free

you   black   out   the   sun

tho   eye   see   clearly   you

come out your pale blue wrap

around   the sky/

so bright   a blind   spot

only the pale bottoms of your feet

whisper   where

you been walking

the clouds   in

the old grandmother's dreaming

hair/

i know where you been.

the ash of lightning shows

above the high heels   your hills

behind the thin rain of your stockings.
i find out where you been
from the shoes that forget/
the meat
of your feet   i love
you   you
been home   been home

IV song about the order of this and the next song

the hump of the sun rottens the berries
the halo wider than ripeness
the fur of the bear staggers
when her shoulder moves / the hump of the sun.

i am a horny man
struggling with a hump
struggling the salmon pause
on the hump   of the air / on my back.

i am the man berry
struggling with the hump of the sun
struggling   the earth flies
on the wine of my skin   the hump of the sun.

i do not sit in your mouth
   to take your beauty.
do not let your tongue poison me.
i will not leave your mouth
   dry of words.
do not shut your sharp teeth on my pen.
i will not stench your mouth
      with my starvation.
do not drink the last of my blood.
do not sew the pussy of your mouth
      closed with lies
here i learn the dowry of my own words.

bored. confused actually. have started several letters.
usually about   4 in the morning wch is to say something
about my tenantcy in the house of sleep/black.
evicted. universal. wch is to say 'There's a certain
                                        amount of traveling
wch is to say   in a dream deferred.'
i taught Langston Hughes today. Same In Blues.
and my soul/*stoppt before the mirror at my body sleeping in the white-
    ness of the moon . . . .*

brought it back.saved   newspaper then lost it
waking up.about the confrontation hate
the loss of meaning in that word) between the black
students and the president   of the campus the folks made him
look like a fool. he is   retreating into his power bag
more jab about in loco parentis do you dig it tsk tsk

there is something about music in this letter. mmm how you do me
this heh way. but the lecture was music   you know
i got so many bags i can only read they faces
from inside.run out   of labels even fore
i run me out of words   wch is to say
/descriptions   there's that refrain again
wch of the wch ways to gone   and say . . .   /black

a classical problem lawd
i/s here by mysef
got no company.what i got
/i
already got.what i know
i know
why i bother with puttin it down.nuthin
nobody else know   wch is to say.
all you all/you people why you want it down   this way
i was about to attend a sinkin.when yall showed up with the hole . . .
mmmiss you baby

you ask was it all right. i said yes wch is to say.
i didn't say (to you no.no is not
a pill.quinine nor enovid.yes is.for me.
tastes weird as anything else
about us. put a hair
on my hope maybe my chest. but thas oright.
been loving other men's sons lately
buying toys for students' sons on my way to dinner
don't take much to get an A from me.
hey hey you there baby at the end of this line
let me be yo sidetrack till yo mainline come
i can do more switchin than yo mainline
done now   students about presumption.'A certain
                                   amount of nothing
1 Ibid.,   in a dream deferred.'
2 vid., next refrain.
3 ad int./cf., today is a ♀ . sine loco(:op.cit.,
4 i.e.,i am   watering an irish rose.   ooop pop a dop bop

i've lost the letter of this act.
with a pun as multiple as that.
"theys liable to be confusion."
to write   a love letter for someone else
to you the one i love
is a love   in a where someworld sometime else
done now
so signed if this is the night, who else but but
is it   black
but look/here look here one more
thing.every new love adds   to the meaning of love any lingering love old love
has to catch up even to linger. so you're going to have
his black baby

i know about the woods you know.
you know i knew the bark who was the sun.
i thought was me.
the rough around the bodies of the oars.
i know how to say the things you know.
you know i never had a whole lot to say.
what i won't leave my sons about carving
was never in the mind of wood.

you know i know how you sleep you know.
i know how to
i know you got to   have 1
i know how my 2   keep me awake.
never one when one numbers the shore of order.
i know what   about myself   you know.
and what my eyes don't look like in the water
never hunted the night.

i know simply   you know
enough to be caught skipping backwards
the smooth stone in a mountain   over no river
without surprise or move   from state to state.
i know the wood simply
the tree is   a wreck   of the ash of the watchfire
what i know that is not a stranger
was never in the mind of order.   of the woods.

1
you will not be even once allowed
to erase   exactness is your eyes
what you cannot see do not record
as none   any mistakes in size
of said must stand as where you are

2
this is the first elimination.
this is the largest elimination
not for the loss at this point
but many are lost here after all
of the other graces are centered
and this is the point.
they are lost here
and now.   all those
who answered pharoah—
              or cherokee . . . .

3
this is nostalgia othellonot grace.
you were not sold a ticket home
from italy why
shld you mourn a true grace
your monkey suit was not on that titanic
why shld you weep
you come from   a better coming you know
i can tell you   this is about the judgement   now
that it is time to speak the language
at hand   that you have lost the came wch
leaves   you free to have the proper moons
you will not be even once allowed
to erase

4

there is nothing you have not
already been exposed to
some in different states
at the various reigns of heat
"A kind of witchdoctor told us that a name is the same name
that has a property."
today the addresses of hydrogen
open the zoo
ological gardens of ologicals
upon you this is less than nothing
some indifferent states

5

history and chauvinisme
art and the functioning gentleman
scientiful thought and the nigger calling called.
the losses.
wch brings us to metaphysical hope
beautiful evidence of even the most ordained
physical evidence of even the most insane
in/the way   they come/from   they stand
one hand in death and in the other life

6

you live in the pan who are maligned with balance
you live the wgt whose counter lies   off fulcruming.
in the light against darkness you never light the cross
your face the sun of night   what you cannot see.
in the cutting off of hands you never left the body
your left hand is black   do not record as none.
any mistakes in size   you fit
the physical evidence of even the most insane
them or me bang

70

                    7
you
look around you look how many of you
how many deaths you have died
that have brought you to life.

fear is fear that the first death
impresses itself too long
on the water
            on the rest
            of this i must ride

on the water
you must let me ride   i know it

the light is in   the way of my feet
the pain is in/   more than the toe.
the limp was born in the darkness
the limp was young in the darkness.
it is a man i come across
it is a man who stumbles
it is a dark man who stumbles on the light.
it is a black man who limps
meanly up behind
the throat of death
who is walking bodies in the park.

i paid my becoming well not to become.
and now gain even to gain my life
's a hole in the hungry pocket of my skin.
and all points between those two are points
opened in that skin and closed there one way:
and any shot   either life or last of thieves
's the opposite of bleeding . and not healed
and not you i am the sieve and not your friend.

i paid my becoming   well   not to   become
i paid
i paid my becoming
      my becoming
                    well
      my becoming well
i paid my becoming well not to
i paid my becoming well not to become.
and now gain even to gain my life
and now
and now gain
          gain even to gain
                even to gain my life
and now gain
's a hole
    a hole in the hungry pocket
              the hungry
                            gain
's a hole in the hungry pocket of my skin.

and all points between those two are points
and all points
and all points between those two
and all points between those two are points
points opened
opened in that skin
opened in that skin and closed there
opened in that skin and closed there
                                        one way!
opened in that skin and closed there one way.
the opposite of bleeding   one way:
and any shot   either life or last of thieves
's the opposite of bleeding

is the opposite of bleeding and not healed
                        and not healed
and not you
            i am the sieve
and not you
            i am the sieve
                        and not healed
and not you i am the sieve
                        and not your friend.
            i am the sieve
                        and not healed
and not you i am the sieve and not your friend.
            i am the sieve and not your friend.
            i am the sieve
            i am the sieve

James Den Boer, *Learning the Way*
  (1967 U.S. Award of the International Poetry Forum)
Jon Anderson, *Looking for Jonathan*
John Engels, *The Homer Mitchell Place*
Samuel Hazo, *Blood Rights*
David P. Young, *Sweating Out the Winter*
  (1968 U.S. Award of the International Poetry Forum)
Fazıl Hüsnü Dağlarca, *Selected Poems*
  (Turkish Award of the International Poetry Forum)
Jack Anderson, *The Invention of New Jersey*
Gary Gildner, *First Practice*
David Steingass, *Body Compass*
Shirley Kaufman, *The Floor Keeps Turning*
  (1969 U.S. Award of the International Poetry Forum)
Michael S. Harper, *Dear John, Dear Coltrane*
Ed Roberson, *When Thy King Is A Boy*

The text and display types used in this
book are Times Roman, a modern roman letter
designed and cut for the *London Times*. The
book is printed directly from the type on
Warren's Olde Style Antique Wove paper, and
bound in Columbia cloth. The design is
by Gary Gore.